Letter Zimbabwe

Written by Anne O'Brien

Africa

Zimbabwe

Celebration Press

Parsippany, New Jersey

Dear Stan and Jessica,

Last week we took a bus to Great Zimbabwe, the Great Stone Place. Our country was named for it. The land around it looks like this.

Long, long ago, ancestors of the Shona lived here. They built all these amazing walls. Zimbabwe is a Shona word. It means house of rock. This is probably where the king lived.

Nothing holds the stones together. Yet the walls have been standing for more than a thousand years!

1,000+

Inside the walls is this stone tower. It's solid rock all the way through, and it's very tall. No one knows for sure what it was used for.

From the walls we could see the Hilltop. It just looked like a bunch of rocks on top of a hill.

But when we climbed up, we found more walls there! It's just like a castle on the hill!

From the Hilltop, we could see far, far across the land. People who lived here could see if anyone was coming.

They all could go up the hill to be safe. Now they are gone, and no one knows why.

When we climbed back down, we went to get a snack. We saw this monkey. It climbed in through the snack bar window. Then it grabbed a snack and ran up into the tree!

Visiting Great Zimbabwe
makes us proud of our
country's history.
We wish you could see it!
Love,

Tsitsi and Tafara